THE
SANDBAG
THEORY

THE
SANDBAG
THEORY

A Collection of Poetry
and Spoken Word

PJ

PHOENIX JAMES

THE SANDBAG THEORY

First Edition: 2024

ISBN: 978-1-7394810-3-2 (Paperback)
ISBN: 978-1-7394810-4-9 (Ebook)

Cover Artwork & Design by Phoenix James.
Book Design & Formatting by Phoenix James.

Visit the author's website at www.PhoenixJamesOfficial.com or email him at phoenix@PhoenixJamesOfficial.com

DEDICATION

To those currently trying to liberate and
free themselves from the shackles of any
form of pain, darkness or despair

Those garnering the strength and courage
to fight on and rise up triumphantly from
being held down as a captive of fear

To all courageously peeling away the
hidden layers of themselves to finally reveal
all of the parts that most are afraid to show

To each one at last mustering the words
they desperately need to share and help
shed themselves of the burden of their past

May this serve to make your load lighter
And your way ahead much clearer

And to a brave young boy, who is forever
with me - and often way, way ahead of me
Here's another one, for us stoke the fire
with - and keep it burning incessantly
I hope it continues to rage endlessly in you
As you are what keeps it raging in me
And I'm sure you know already, but the
journey is really about to heat up and take
off from here - hope I'm as ready as you are
And I hope seeing this, warms your heart.

CONTENTS

ABSTAINING IS THE NEW SEX

I don't want any relationship
Or any social construct of marriage
And what relationships are supposed to be
It's just waste of time and energy
I don't want that socially constructed stuff
I want that normal stuff human beings do
Which is have sex and stuff
But getting married and all of that
That's something that someone devised
Oh let's just get married
And do this and do that
No, I don't believe in that
I do believe in marriage of the mind
Body, soul, spirit, and all of that
I believe in that kind of marriage
But not marriage like let's go buy a dress
And order a cake
And get a suit
And invite all these people
And have a big ceremony
I don't believe in that
I believe in, if I want to have sex
And have sexual needs
I have that

With someone who is consenting
In the same way
And happy to do that as well
And I've met that need
I don't need to marry someone
To have sex
That's number one
Not interested at all
In fact, that's all
That's one and all
Have sex when I need it
Have companionship when I need it
When I need company or friends
If I need feminine energy
In an intimacy way
Then it'll be a female
If I don't, then it won't
Then it'll be whatever
But not to have someone
Friends with benefits
Even that's become a social construct now
It's like, this is the arrangement
This is the marriage arrangement
Or marriage agreement
This is the friends with benefits agreement
And arrangement

That's become even a thing now
Where like, you probably
Should have a contract for that now
If you're friends with benefits
Because what one person thinks
Is friends with benefits
The other person might not
That's not on the list
No, I didn't say that
I didn't agree
I didn't agree to anal
No matter how much
Friends we are with benefits
Nope, not doing that
No, that's not going in there
Friends with benefits
That just seems like another thing
I like to think of it more loosely
Because today
Friends with benefits now
Is like a marriage
It's like a contract
Like, it has to be this way
It's expected that this happens
Or that happens
It's just becoming mad

Abstaining might be
The best thing overall
Staying away from the whole lot
Abstaining is the new sex
Yeah, man
Abstinence
Keep it under your skirt
And keep it in your pants
Keep it in your knickers
Keep it in your pants
That's the key to a happy life.

AVOIDING UNWANTED ADVANCES

Me, I'm being a good boy
I'm converting to the church
And giving my life to Christ
And cannot engage in certain activities
That would be against my faith
Fornication being top of the list
I focus my eyes on my saviour now
I give over all my desires
And things of the world
Worldly things
I give them up
And live a life of godliness
Yeah
Celibacy is my focus now
Abstinence.

BLINDFOLD ME

I'd be blindfolded
Yeah, I would do that
I'm not sure about tying up though
I'm not sure about being tied up
But a blindfold
Yeah, I would do the blindfold thing
Because again
It's like coming back to sensuality
And being sensuous
And touch
I think it'd be quite exciting
Not to know
Where the next touch is coming from
Absolutely
It's that whole thing
It adds to it doesn't it
Not knowing
Where you're going to be touched next
And all the sensitivity
It's just great
One hundred-percent
Yes
Give me a blindfold.

CHIPS FOR BEANS

Absolutely
Do you know how I think it will start
This is just a crazy theory
I just came up with in my head
But I feel
It will be like circumcision
That's how the discussion will be
How people talk about circumcision now
Are you circumcised
Are you not circumcised
I feel that's how it will be
With being chipped
Were you chipped at birth
Or were you not chipped
That'd be the conversation
Some people would expect it
Like the injections for school
Immunisation
I think in terms of monitoring people
Down the line
Keeping control of things
I think it'll be the only way
Chip everybody
Chip you at birth

It'll be like that
Like your injections
It'll be, have you had your chip
And you'll know exactly what it is
You'll just know
That you need to go and do it
Once you're chipped
You can get these beans.

CURVY WINS EVERYTHING

I like any woman's size
Once it's curvy
Once she's shapely
Has a curviness to her
Like, remember Jessica Rabbit
From the Roger Rabbit movie
Like, the curves she had in the cartoon
The Coca Cola bottle shape, whatever
As long as a woman has that shape
She could be any size
She could be as big
As Stay Puft Marshmallow Man
From Ghostbusters
Yeah, she could be that size
Remember, big, massive
Walking through the city
Terrorising everybody
Yeah, she could be that big
As long as she's got the shape
That curviness to her
As long as she's got
The Coca Cola bottle shape going on
She could be tiny as ever
Or she could be as massive as ever

As long as she's got the shape there
Oh, hell yeah it's sexy
One hundred precent
I don't care how big she is
If she's curvy, I'm involved
Or small
Even if she's small
But she's curvy with it
Yeah, I'm down
You can't beat curvy, man
Big or small
Curvy wins
Curvy just wins
Curvy wins over everything.

DON'T OVERTHINK IT

The only danger is
Sometimes
We read, we read, we read
We learn, we learn, we learn
We try to understand
We try to figure out
Before we make a step
Before we make a move
And then before we know it
We haven't done anything
And sadly a lot of the time passes
The moment to execute
To do, to seize, to jump on
We spent so much time
Trying to be perfect
Before we start
Rather than making a move
And learning as we go along
That's a danger sometimes
Of so much study and pondering
And trying to figure out
And be perfect
Sometimes, you just have to go.

ENJOY YOUR LIFE, DON'T WASTE IT

I was talking to a friend this evening
Which reminded me of some thoughts
I was having this morning
And basically
I was thinking
If you're like forty plus years old now
If you look at how quickly that time went
You realise, it was like a blink of an eye
Like twenty to thirty went quick
Then thirty to forty went even quicker
It's like to say, if you live
You've got roughly another forty years
Older people say
That it goes quicker and quicker
The older you get
So your forty to fifty
Goes even quicker than thirty to forty
And then fifty to sixty goes even quicker
Than forty to fifty, and so on
It's like a blink of an eye
So imagine how quick
The next forty will go
If we are blessed with another forty
It's like we don't have fucking time

To waste, really
We don't have time to waste
Sweating on shit that doesn't really matter
That's just putting it bluntly
We're gone tomorrow
We're gone in a second
Our existence is so minuscule
In the great scheme of things
What a blessing it is
To even have seen this shit
What a blessing it is
To even have existed in the first place
We were the sperm that made it
To even be here now
Having this conversation
Interacting with each other in this way
We are the sperms that fucking made it
And we fucking waste so much time
On trivial shit
And things that don't even matter
Things that are just irrelevant
Things that are not even worth the time
When you look at the special time
That we have here
And what we get to experience
In the time that we have on earth

And how brief it is
It's fucking crazy
How much time we ponder
And waste time worrying
About shit that won't even matter
In a year's time or six months time
Or in a week's time
We just get so caught up
That next forty
For those of you who are forty like me
And plus
We don't have much time
We don't have another forty
To spend our lives worrying
About bullshit and crap
That other people worry about
Seriously
We don't, we just don't
Time wasting, time wasting
Do not waste time, people
Do not waste your life away
Even if you're twenty, thirty
Sixteen or whatever
Know that your time goes so damn quick
It just goes, it goes so quick, man
Enjoy your life

14

Maximise your life
Make the most of it
And enjoy every moment
Don't worry about stuff
That doesn't even really matter
In the grand scheme of things
When you're on your deathbed
And in those last moments
You think about what you enjoyed
Don't let it be regrets
About time that you wasted
Worrying about trivial shit
Like relationships that didn't work out
And hating people for the rest of your life
Carrying that hate and that grievance
All that stuff
Just out the window
Forget it
Today
Because that's all we have
All we have is today
Do not waste your life
Live your life
Have a good time
Whatever you're doing
I mean, just enjoy your life, man

Just enjoy your life
And maximise the time
That you have here
You don't have it long
I'm not going to be here for that long
You're not going to be here for that long
It goes in a blink of an eye
This is all we have right now
Do not waste it
Enjoy your life.

EVENING PLANS

I could do with my coat right now
But I've just been lazy to put it on
It's been a warm day
It's been a t-shirt day for real
It's been good, even now
Slight chill as the sun has gone down
And it's getting late
But it's still relatively warm
Considering what it could be
It's not too bad, not too bad
I'm going to chill out for a little bit
And then I'm going to go home
And look to get some rest, chill out
I'm quite tired actually
But the fresh air has woken me up again
So I don't know
I haven't fully decided yet what I'll do
But not planning to stay up too late
I've got some bits to do
So I'd like to make a move
To get to bed at a decent hour
That's the plan
Who knows
I may end up staying up late

Watching TV with mother dearest
Which has been known to happen
On occasion, many occasions
That's not a bad thing
But my Monday nights
And Tuesday nights
Are reserved for TV watching
So I kind of have to ration myself
I can't, you know, overdo it
I have two particular TV series
That I've just started watching
So once I've watched those
I've kind of maxed out
On my TV watch-time allowance
We'll see what transpires
If there's anything on the box
That I catch mother dearest watching
And I think looks interesting.

EVERYONE'S GOT THEIR OWN SHIT

Some people
Are just in a messed up place, man
Some people are just not in a good place
And sometimes we forget
That where they're at
Is not where you're at sometimes
And their behaviour
And things they may say, actions
Reasons they have for doing things
Are based on the fact
That they're not in a good place
And sometimes
We have to try to bear that in mind
We have to realise
That people are acting off of
Where they're at
The limited information
They may have at that time
And try to put yourself in their shoes
And see those things
It's not always clear cut
Why this person is like this
Sometimes
There's other things going on

With a person
And will affect how they behave
It's easy to forget that sometimes
Hard at times to stomach
But easier to deal with
When you realise
That not everyone is where you're at
And they're dealing with their own shit
Everyone's dealing with their own shit
Sometimes you forget
That you're not the only one with shit
Or when your shit is not so bad
That other people may still be in bad shit
So everyone is not where you're at, basically
You just have to kind of
See with people sometimes
Their experience of life in general
May be different from yours
And the way they process information
The way they handle situations
The way they don't handle situations
It's all coming from a place
That you may not be in
And that's basically the gist of this
What I'm talking about
What I'm expressing

Sometimes you have to kind of
Be outside of yourself
And look at things
From an outside perspective of why
Someone has the actions they have
Or has the thoughts they have
Or why they're acting
The way they're acting
It's a lot easier
When you're able to do that
Easier said than done
But when you do that
It's a lot easier to deal with
The stuff that people throw at you
They may be throwing things at you
That have nothing to do with you
Whatsoever
It's easy to forget
Be outside of yourself sometimes
When things are going on
And without your own thoughts
About things sometimes
Just step outside
Of your own mind sometimes
And just think
As hard as it may be

That not everyone is you
And they're acting
Based on
The limited information
They have at that time
Yeah, life
People, things, experiences.

GAMBLING MAN

I just need to talk about
This guy right now
I'm sitting next to a slot machine
And he came in
He was on it
I don't know how much
He put in the first time
He was paying for a little while
So he must have put
A certain amount of money in
I didn't realise
That with these slot machines
You can put paper money into it to play
This is news to me
I never knew that
I'm coming from thc cra
Where you put coins in and you play
So this guy
I saw him take out his wallet
And he's putting in notes
The first was a twenty pound note
That he put into the machine
And then he's playing on, he's playing on
Then he goes into his wallet again

He puts in a ten pound note
He's playing, he's playing
He goes to his wallet again
He puts in another ten pound note
He goes to his wallet again
He puts in another ten pound note
And this guy has spent fifty pounds
Well that's the bit I saw
I didn't see what he started with
And he was there a good while
Before I noticed
That he'd actually gone into his wallet
To get out paper money
This is the new world, man
That was in a space of like eight minutes
Or let's call it ten to be fair
In ten minutes he put fifty pounds in
I don't know how much
He put in before that
And he hasn't won anything
He didn't win anything at all
And he looks like
He's just coming from work
And he's come in this bar here
And he's gone to the slot machine
I don't even think he's bought a drink

He's just come straight to the machine
And given it fifty pounds, or more
Well, definitely more
Wow, that's an expensive game
If you're into playing games
And just want to play a bit of gambling
It's expensive to play
It's an expensive hobby, man, wow
Since when could you put paper money
Into a slot machine
I never knew this
You can tell I'm not a gambler, right
I'm a gambling man only when
I know I'm going to win
You can't even say, gamble responsibly
Like you say, drink responsibly
It's like, fuck man
You get hooked, right
You can't gamble responsibly
You can't say, I'm going to go
And just spend fifty today
I'll be good with that
I'll spend twenty pound
It's fine if I don't win anything
It's not like that
It's the thrill of it

It's like a chase
You want it, you want it, you want it
I can win, I can win, I can win
And you keep going
Until like, fuck, man
Until you've lost your whole life
Car, house, wife, children
The whole lot
All gambled away
Down the drain
Job, everything
Fuck, man, crazy
Borrowing money to continue playing
I was just looking at him
Just gambling away
He didn't win a thing
The machine has profited
He didn't even buy a drink
He didn't come in here
To buy a drink at all
He came straight to the machine
Gave it his money and left
That was his fix
And he didn't get what he needed from it
Maybe he needs to win
And he's going to continue doing that

Until he gets something back
Hopefully the stakes go in his favour
At some point
But then, when it does that
That's the hook
Because then you think
You could do that again
That you can replicate that win
And then you lose it all again
I bet that was his reason
For being here
He felt lucky
Wow
Yeah, man
It's a crazy game.

GETTING HER WET BEFORE SEX

Some people are just scared of the water
You just have to literally pick them up
And throw them in the tub or shower
And drag them in kicking and screaming
If you want them to actually be clean
Jesus man, some adults are just frowsy
And want to sleep with you
And haven't had a wash
In I don't know how long
It's true
I'm all about the cleanliness
All about the cleanliness
Especially if it's someone
You're not familiar with
I've said this before
You need to go and wash
If it's the first time we're meeting
Or hooking up
Or things might happen
Be clean
Fuck that
Don't even think about it
If you've been walking around all day
Or sitting around all day

And haven't had a shower
And you're going to meet someone
Forget it
It's not going to happen
I'm just talking about the cleanliness
It's respectful, you know
On both sides
To have a shower and be clean
And presentable
This subject can't get enough airplay
Wash your damn self
Before you go around people
Wanting to get naked and get down
Where are you going
I'm not one to accept it
The amount of women in my time
I've had to drag kicking and screaming
Into the showcr
What happened to those women
That are self conscious and insecure
And worried
About what the man might think
Or say
These frowsy women are like, wow
Don't care.

HOW DO YOU KNOW IT'S REALLY LOVE?

My definition of love is
Some kind of deep feeling
You may have with someone
Or something
Some emotion attached to a person
Or a thing that you care for
I think that's the thing
Knowing whether you are or not
I think those emotions and feelings
Can be confused
To be love
But not be love
Someone could say
I love this cake
This ice cream
And then I can say
I love the person
Or 'I love you' to somebody
I think the lines can be blurred
I think it's quite a loose term
That people use
People say, they love people
But do they really love them
Is it a real love

People talk about love
Being this all conquering thing
This impenetrable force
If you really love someone
You wouldn't do this, or that
I don't know
I'm still figuring it out
The definition and what it means
The thing is
Have I ever had it
I don't know
I actually don't know
If I've ever had it
That's the truth
I don't know
I can say, I felt like I was in love
At this point, or that point, in my life
But I can't say for sure
If that was what I was feeling it
Or was I just infatuated by this person
Was it lust
What was it
Was it really love
Or was it addiction
How do you know when it's love
That's the question

How do you know
I don't know
I'll tell you something
I've heard that when it hits you
When you are in love
You know
You know when you are
That's what I've heard
It might be hogwash
But I've heard that
That's what all the love songs say.

HOW I LIKE TO DO IT

It depends on my mood
I'm not like the guy
Who's going to throw you
All over the room
And bash your head
And rip your clothes off
Like literally rip them off
And you can't actually use them anymore
At the same time
I'm not like
The flowery guy
I say flowery as an example of soft
Like marshmallows soft
I'm that as well
I'm a combination of both
But I'll probably take your clothcs off
As opposed to rip them
And I'll probably
Lean you up against the wall
As opposed to throw you
I'll reach the parts
But I won't do it to the point
That you might not be able to walk
For a week

Unless you specifically ask for that
I mean, maybe that's
Something we could talk about
But I wouldn't impale you in that way
I would actually reach the parts
In a more slower, sensual way
Because I'm that kind of guy
So I'm kind of both
I can be really soft
And really hard at the same time
And mix the two
Come into the middle
With them both mixed
A nice balance of sensuality
And lovemaking
And climax
And orgasmic stuff going on
I like to do the massage beforehand
Loosen up everything
Get the oils going on
And the right environment
And the right vibe
And the music and all that
I'm that guy
I'm the soft, marshmallow
Flowery guy in that way

But then when I'm getting down
I want to make sure
I'm hitting everything
I'm connecting with your soul.

HOW I RESPOND TO PROBLEMS

I process the situation
I weigh up the pros and cons
And think about how
It would impact on me
If I went this way
Or how it would impact on me
If I went that way
I think about what I've learned
Growing up
How would my gran look at it
Little things like that cross my mind
I think about my mentors
And things I've learned from them
Processing that information
How can I use that
What have I learned
Through NLP, that can help me
To deal with this situation
I always take a moment
To ponder or pause
And look at where I am
And how I'm looking at the situation
Am I making the situation
Bigger than it is

Am I overthinking it
Sometimes
I'll go away and leave a thing
If it's something
That's on my head in that way
Where I feel perhaps, stressed out by it
I take a moment
And just think about where I'm at
And ask, how important is this really
And when you do that
It makes those things quite small
It can make those things smaller
Than they are initially
When they're initially in your face
I tend to go through those processes
If it's a lot, if it's like a big thing
I will look at what's positive
About the situation
I'll do that
And I will step away for a moment
Just to reflect
What I don't do
Is react instantly
Straight away
Without pause for thought
That is one thing I've learned

How am I allowing this to affect me
What is this really
That kind of thing
Have I blown it out of proportion
Will it matter tomorrow
Next week, next year
I go through those processes of thought
I refer to things I've learned
About how to deal with the situation
I kind of lean on my own understanding
Although, that may not always
Be the best way to go
But it's not only my own understanding
It's my own understanding
From things from other people
So I'm talking about my mentors
And things I've learned from them
So I'd go through that process
What would they do in this situation
I know people have their friends
They call up
And their mates they speak to
I'm just not that way
I'm just not wired that way
I don't know if it's part of growing up
As an only child

Or always moving around a lot
And not having
A massive friendship base in that way
It's always been quite tight
So I've had to make a lot of decisions
And process a lot of things on my own
Just the nature
Of the way my life has been
So I tend not to
Bring things to friends
But through mentors
I will think about
What would such and such do
In this situation
What would they say about this
How would they
Talk about handling this
And I'll refer to that
And that will help me think about it
If my own thoughts of it
Are not enough
Or I feel I need more
I'll go that route
I'll think about
What would The A-Team do
In this situation.

I ALMOST BECAME A MALE PROSTITUTE

Yes, I was going to be an escort
At one point in my life
And I still may, who knows
I only came across the idea of it
Because I met a guy at an event
We were modelling together
And he told me he's an escort as well
And he was earning sometimes
Eight hundred pounds at a time
I thought, Wow
That sounds pretty good
Compared to what we're getting right now
For this modelling gig
I think we were at the V&A Museum
Or somewhere, I can't remember
He was doing that on the side
And he was going to give me some contacts
I didn't pursue it, I didn't chase it
But I thought that's not bad money
To make for a few hours work
He says he didn't have to have sex
With all the women
It was his choice
Whether or not he wanted to have sex

It was that type of thing
It was some exclusive agency
He was with
And he would go out
And meet these people
And sometimes
They just wanted someone
On their arm
To go to their events with
To be present
For some company, or whatever
You know, tall, good looking
Six foot, black guy
Shaved head going on at the time
And he would go out with these women
It wasn't always about sex
I can't remember now
IIow much of it was sexual
But I do remember
That it wasn't always based on sex
Some people just wanted to go out
And it would be more money
If they wanted to have sex as well
As part of the arrangement
I just didn't pursue it, I didn't chase it
But I could have

And still could if I wanted to
I'm actually only thinking about it now
That I'm talking about it
But I don't think it's something
That interests me to do
Could I have sex with someone
That I didn't really fancy, for money
Well, I've had sex with people
That I didn't fancy
Just for the pleasure of it
Just because it was me wanting to
Get my end away, as they call it
You know, just for the release
So if I was doing that
And getting paid
I think I could probably do it
Thinking okay, I'm doing this
But I'm getting money
I can do this
I mean, I used to do this anyway
For zero money
So yeah, I probably could
But I haven't thought about it
In a long time
Until this conversation
It's funny.

I CAN SEE WHAT SHE'S WORKING WITH

I don't know why
I don't know why that is, at all
I couldn't tell you why
I mean, nature of man, and female species
And all that kind of stuff
I don't know why it is
I've got a friend
A heterosexual, hot blooded male like me
Him not so much
As he's now a married man
But as we are
You know, men
Male species
He would see a woman approaching
And he would see her breasts first
Me, I would see her hips
I'm a bum and thigh man
He's a breast man
He will see her breasts first
And I would see her hips
And her thighs
And her bum
You're probably wondering
How I see her bum from the front

But the funny thing is
I can kind of tell
What a woman is working with
From the front
How, by the way she walks
And carries herself
By the weight of her steps
The way she moves
The way her structure is
I can kind of tell
What's going on behind
From the front
Just the way she walks
Just the way her footsteps are
Whether they're heavy or not
I can kind of tell what's going on
And that's even
If she's wearing a long coat
Buttoned up
One hundred percent
And that's just by
Nothing more than
Just by observing women
You can generally tell
What you're seeing
What's there

You've got a pretty good gauge
Of what's going on behind
From the front
When a woman
Is walking towards you
It's all to with
The weight of her body
How she moves
Has she got really light steps
Does she move really fast
Does she move swift on her feet
Does she walk more slowly
Like she's carrying stuff behind her
So it's to do with that
Just how she moves
That's all it's about
Also, I can kind of tell
From her face as well
Not as easily, but can kind of tell
For example, if she's quite cheeky
In her face
You can kind of tell
That she's going to be
Quite cheeky behind her as well
If her forearms
Are relatively thick

You can kind of tell
That she's thick all around
Judging by her wrist area
Up to her elbow
I can tell you a good example
That displays it quite well
The film, Ray
About singer-songwriter
And pianist
Ray Charles
Starring the actor Jamie Foxx
There's a scene in the film
Obviously he's blind
He's introduced to a woman
And he feels her arm
They make reference to it
In the movie
That he can tell
What she's got going on
In other words
What her physique is like
Just from feeling her forearm
That's exactly what I'm talking about
That's a good example
That's the same with me
And I can kind of tell that

From her face as well
And her arms
I can kind of tell
What's going on elsewhere
If that's all I had to go on
If I was blind
I could tell
What her physique might be like
By doing the same thing.

I DESPISE THE FAIRYTALE SOME DAYS

I don't want to get married
I'm not in a hurry to get married
I always say I like the idea
I'm the boy of the fairytale
I love the idea
I love what we grew up with
I love watching the shows
Where the boy saves the girl
And they go off and get married
And live happily ever after
And have all the kids
I just don't see it for myself anymore
I do and I don't
I see it
But the reality
Is very far from it
I just really don't see it being a thing
Like a real thing
And having kids again
And going through all the politics
And all the downside
Of relationships
And having children
In relationships

That don't work out
It's one of the things
I don't want to have to deal with
To be honest with you
You get to a certain age
And you just
Don't want to go through it
And you think
Why should you.

I LOVE MYSELF

I love myself
I've been told to say
I love myself
I've been tested
And told
That I wouldn't say
I love myself
And I wouldn't put it out
Or put it up anywhere
But I love myself
And I'm proud to say
I love myself
I'm not waiting
For anyone to love me
I love myself
Therefore I'm open to love
From anybody else
And anything else
Because I love myself first
I feel no way to say it
To express it
Yes, I love myself
Okay, there it is
It's on the record

I love myself
In fact, this is called
I love myself
I hope you love yourself too.

IF I WAS IN POWER

I think if I was in power
And I was in a place
Where I could choose
Between telling my subjects
The truth
And lying to them
I like to think
I would pride myself
On being a truth teller
Telling them the truth
And priding myself
On being the one
Who tells the truth
The one who tells it how it is
And not being in a place
Where I'm afraid
To tell them the truth
Because, why
They won't follow me anymore
They won't listen to me anymore
I feel I could equally attain
Or keep, or maintain
My reign
Or my success

Or my throne
Or whatever it is
By telling the truth
Because they know
This is the man
That speaks the truth
We want to follow him
We want our eyes opened
This is the man to follow
So, I think in essence
It would make me even greater
Do I think I could handle
Being in power
I think it's a lot of responsibility
I like to think that I could
I wouldn't want to think
That I couldn't ever be in power
Or not be enough of a person
Within myself
Whatever attributes
Or whatever things
That make a good leader
Or a good person in power
I'd like to think
That I have what it takes
I wouldn't say otherwise

I do believe that I do
I know there are things
That may be required of me
That I'd have to learn going forward
That I might not have now
But I like to think
I'd be a great leader
And I have what it takes
If I was fortunate to have that position
Or was placed in that position of power
I would implement abstinence
Times where the act of sex
Is not practised
I believe there's so much good in that
When things are not driven
By the act of sex
Or the desire for sex
I think when that's taken away
And people have to focus
On other things
Other than this emotion
Or desire
That drives so many of us
I think a lot would come out of that
As individuals
I think we would grow so much from that

I don't know how I would do it
I don't know how I would implement it
But I know there would be a way
To enforce it
I don't want to use the word enforce
I don't want to use the word inspire either
But a way to bring that about
Where that is practiced
I don't want to say like a religion either
Or like a cult
Or anything like that
But that's one of the things
I would push for
Times of abstinence
Where the act of sex
Physical sex
Is not practised
I have no idea how it would work
But I know once it was in motion
And it was working
I know the benefits
That would come from it
For individuals
For human beings
For the mindset of us as a people
I'd have a lot of opposition

But I'd go for it anyway
I like to think
That I could present
A valuable strong case
For why it makes sense
I know it would be met with opposition
I know I'd be called a looney
I know I'd be called mad
And other stuff
But I still at the same time
Believe I could present
A strong case
For why it's necessary
For the advancement of mankind
Times of abstinence.

IF YOU COULD GO BACK

I have a question for you
If you had the opportunity
To go back
To a certain period of your life
Would you
And if you did
Would you change anything
Would you go back
Just to experience
The experience again
Or would you be going back
To change something
That you want to change.

IN KNOWING THYSELF, KNOW THIS

I feel, knowing yourself
Is an ongoing process
I feel like you don't fully
Know yourself, ever
I think you're on a constant
Ongoing road to knowing yourself
I think you'll know yourself
A little bit better each time
As you go along
But there's always
Something unravelling
Where you surprise yourself
You didn't know you were like that
Or you didn't know you thought like that
You didn't know you could do that
I don't think that ever changes
And I like that
That kind of keeps it exciting
Imagine you get to the point in life
Where you just know yourself
I mean, there's knowing yourself
There's a degree to knowing yourself
Which is like the general standard
You know, as in, I know myself

But you're always
Learning new stuff about yourself
And you should be
Because everything else
Is changing around you
Why would you not be changing
We're always evolving
So we're bound to change
With new things to know
And discover about ourselves
And that's the way it should be
We should never reach this point
Of I know myself
And there's no more
That I'm going to learn about myself
That's not real
I've learned so much
About myself this year alone
That I didn't know about myself before
That, for me, has just blown my mind
To be honest with you
Like, wow
I didn't know I could be this way
Or that I thought this way
Or that I had these things inside my mind
Especially doing stuff like this

Where I'm just
Documenting my thoughts
Things come out
That I wasn't even aware of
In the way that they come out
That I was thinking about them
In that way
But they're there
They're inside me
So I know myself
But then I'm learning about myself
At the same time
It's an ongoing process
Going around as we evolve
We change
So our knowledge of ourselves
Should always be changing too
It should be
It can't say, Oh, I know it all now
I know myself now, that's it
There's nothing more
To learn about myself
That sounds crazy
Physically, mentally, spiritually
All of it
Know thyself

Know that you will never
Know yourself completely
Know that you will always
Be changing and evolving
Like everything else around you
Know this.

IS AGE FOUR TOO YOUNG FOR SEX?

I presented the argument
And then I presented
A possible counter argument
That may be presented
To that initial argument
The argument is, that I feel
Teaching sex education
To a four year old
Is way too young
It's just unnecessary
They're just too young
There's just no need
To teach a four year old
About sex at such an early age
That was the argument
The counter argument
That may be presented to that
Is that children now
Are exposed to sex
At such an early age
Without proper guidance
With the internet
iPad, phone, computer
Or whatever it is

And how a parent
Is quick to shove a phone
Or an iPad in the child's hands
To keep it quiet
Or through the child's friends
They're going to have access to it
If they want to
Their friends have got pornography
Everyone's got access, basically
That's the counter argument
To say, well, it might be a good idea
To start teaching them about sex early
So that there's some kind of
Guidance to it
So that it's not just out there
In the wind
And they're just getting this education
From other places
Where it might not be guided properly
The exposure they have to sex
And the internet
And porn, and that whole thing
If there's some kind of
Early education
Then they've kind of been guided
So that when children

Do see those things
They have an understanding
As opposed to
Not having an understanding
And just being presented with this thing
That's alien to them
Sex is a big thing
At any age, really
But especially when you're a four year old
And up, five, six, seven, eight, nine, ten
It's in your face, everywhere
So the counter argument is
Start teaching kids at an early age
And providing them with guidance
To that whole world of sex
Through the proper means
Whatever that is
Rather than just, you know
Them being out there
And exposed to it
Without any
Mental protection, if you like
Against that exposure
When they face it
Not having experienced
What sex is all about

64

So that's the counter argument
To age four being too young
For a child to be educated about sex
Which I personally feel is too young
And it's unnecessary
But then, as I said
That's the counter argument
To that whole thing
So we have the argument
And the counter argument
For the question
Is teaching four year olds
About sex
To young of an age.

KEEPING OUT OF TROUBLE

I told my mum yesterday
I've got to keep myself busy
Got to keep out of trouble
I'm a young black male
From the east end of London, Hackney
That's already going against me
Stereotypically
So I've got to keep myself busy, man
That's against me
So I've got to keep out trouble there
And then there's the women
I'm a six foot tall, dark, handsome guy
Talented and all that kind of stuff
Women are going to be coming in droves
So I've got to keep out of trouble, man
You can get yourself into trouble
With these ladies
So from all angles
I've got to keep out of trouble
It's really serious out here
You've got to watch yourself
There's men too
As I said, handsome guy
Guys that are into guys, see me

And they think, you know
Can something happen there
So you've got to watch yourself all sides
Got to watch yourself
Got to keep out of trouble
You've got to watch your back
You've got to watch your left shoulder
You've got to watch your right shoulder
You've got to watch what's in front of you
You've got to watch what's behind you
It's all sides, man
You've got to watch
You've got to look above as well
Anything could fall on you
That you're not expecting
Troubles could fall on your head
You've got to just watch yourself
You've got to have
Your head on your shoulders
And know what's about you
Just got to keep out of trouble
That's what I said
To my mum yesterday
It's real talk
I said, you've got to
Keep yourself occupied

You've got to find things
To occupy your time
To keep you out of trouble
One of the things I said to her was
The saying, that the devil
Makes work for idle hands
That's the same thing
I was saying yesterday
It's very true
Keeping out of trouble
That's what I'm doing
That's all that's going on right here
Keeping out of trouble.

KNOW YOUR WORTH

People don't realise
How interesting they are
Every individual
Has something interesting
About them
It's just that people
Don't think they're interesting
They look outside
They look in magazines
They look on the TV
They look in the cinema
They look at movies
And it's all big
And it's all grandiose
All the promotion
All the celebrity
Red carpet
And all that stuff
But they don't look in the mirror
And look at their own lives
And look at how amazing they are
How interesting they are
If they really got down to it
If they read a book

About themselves
People would be bowled over
By how interesting they are
How interesting that book is
I wish I could just
Turn a mirror to everyone
Who thinks they're boring
And just let them see themselves
Or read themselves in a book
Or see their lives
Played out in a movie
By an actor
Just to see their lives
They would realise
How interesting they are
How amazing they are
That there's no one like them
In the world
There's no one
Quite like that individual
There's no one like you
In our world
How amazing is that
There is no one person
Exactly like you
There is no one person

On this planet
Exactly like you
You are the only one
You're one copy
There's never going to be another
There's been none before
You're the only one
How amazing is that
You're so fucking special
So special
You're a one-off
There's never going to be
A repeat of you
I wish I could show everyone
A movie of themselves
Played out by a famous actor
Playing them
From young
To how they grew up
And their story
Going to school, all of it
That would be a fascinating movie
For all the people
That think they're uninteresting
I wish I could do that
Or in documentary form

Where they could watch
Their life story
How amazing would that be
I wish I could do that right now
For every person
Who thinks they're boring
And uninteresting
Wouldn't that be great to do
And to show them that it's not true
That you're actually special
You're amazing
You're brilliant
You're everything
There is something
Amazingly interesting
About everybody
Because they're so unique
Because there's only one of them
How could that not be amazing
And interesting
And everything
Other than boring
People are amazing
And they don't even know
How amazing and special
And unique they are.

LANGUAGE OF THE FUTURE

I think
Going back to
The subject
Of our youngsters
Being at a disadvantage
If we don't allow them
To have the freedom
To explore where the world is going
Like the basics
Imagine
You have children now
Who, aside from school
When they have to put pen to paper
Which again, is questionable
A lot of stuff is done on computers now
But like simply writing things down
On a piece of paper
If they're not texting
Or doing it on an iPad
Or a computer screen
They're not used to that
They're not in that habit
Of getting the pen
And paper

And a pencil even
And writing something down
A note, a number, an address
They're just not in that routine
So imagine
When they have to now go
And be without their phone
Or that type of technology
That they're used to so much
They're going to be kind of stuck
Like, how do I write again
How do I spell
Because on a mobile phone
They know exactly where every key is
With their eyes closed
But give them the alphabet
And a pen and paper
And write some words down
They may be a little stuck
I get it saves time
To write the number '2'
Instead of the word 'too'
But it's one of my peeves
In one sense
We've got to kind of respect it
Because they've created a text language

There is a language
That has been created now
Which is your shorthand today
From yesterday's shorthand
Klingon on is a language
Who knows
The way the youngsters are writing now
And a lot of adults too
The way they shorten words
And write numbers
Instead of the actual word
Or they write the letter 'c' instead of 'see'
What will happen in the future
Will people not understand
What the hell that says
Or what that means
Or will it be like
The new form of hieroglyphics
For the future, future
Will people look at it on walls
Or on computers
And understand it
Like this is the ancient language
Or would they be like
What the hell is this
We don't understand this one

We understand this, this is English
We remember this
This is what our ancestors used
Our ancestors spoke English
We understand this
They called this English in their time
We understand this
But what is this other thing here
What is this other language
We don't understand this..
C u l8r
Or is it going to be a derivative
Are they going to look at it as
A derivative from English
It's interesting
We will see, I guess
Time will tell, I should say
Rather than, we will see
Because you and I won't be around.

LAST TIME YOU'LL EVER HEAR FROM ME

I'll tell you a story
About something that occurred to me
And it only hit me later
I was dating this girl
And we fell out
Through no fault of my own
I stopped speaking to her
I just thought she was rude
And due to the way
She handled the situation
I just said
I'm not speaking to this person again
I'm not dealing with her anymore
So that was the nature of it
And that was it
On the last message I sent
I said, this is the last time
You'll ever hear from me
And it only occurred to me
Maybe a year later
That her hearing that from someone
Is not a big deal
The fact that you're taking yourself
Out of this person's life

She was an abandoned child
She grew up with foster parents
Because her parents left her
She was found at a train station
As a baby
So she's grown up
Not knowing her family
Not knowing her parents
Not knowing her mum and dad
So that love
That thing that's kind of missing
From your life
When you're born into that absence
Or a situation like that happens
Abandonment is something you know
It's nothing to you
When someone's leaving your life
When relationships end in your life
You're not that affected by it
I can relate to that
I've never been left at a train station
And I've grown up with my mum
But I know what it's like
To have that feeling of abandonment
I know what it's like to live with that
Not to her degree

But I can see now looking back
That it was no big issue for her
I was walking away
And it wasn't a loss to her
Or maybe it was
I don't know to what degree
But I don't think
It was like someone else
The average person
Would feel that loss
Of missing a person
I feel like she could get over that
Quite easily
Because you become okay
With people leaving
And not being in your life
You become conditioned to it
You kind of expect it
That only occurred to me
A year later
That she probably just
Didn't think anything of it
You know, like it's nothing to her
But to my credit
The way she behaves
I wouldn't be surprised

If a lot of her relationships
Ended in that way
People just ending them basically
And to her credit
Maybe she kind of has this thing
Of pushing people away
Because sometimes
That nature is formed in people
When they're used to
Being in relationships
That don't work out
In some sense as well
If you were left
At train station as a baby
Or on someone's doorstep
Or wherever
That's being born
Into abandonment
So your relationships
Can be shaky
And flaky going forward
And it wouldn't be a big deal
When people leave
That was a couple of years ago now
But only hit me this year
Did I love her

I wouldn't say I loved her
We didn't get to the stage of love
We were still in the process
Of getting to know each other
This is why as things developed
The way they developed
It was a surprise
I was learning
About this new person
How they treat people
And I decided to
Terminate my connection
My relationship
My contact with them
And later realised
That it was no big deal
That they weren't going to
Hear from me again
Because that's like nothing to them
It's a bigger deal if you realise
You're not going to hear
From your family again
Or your mum and dad
I mean, if you're an adult
And your mum and dad
Are abandoning you

At a train station
That's a bigger deal
Than some guy
You just not long ago met
And saw him off and on
Yeah, just occurred to me
No loss to her really
Or me.

LOOSE THOUGHTS ON MENTAL HEALTH

I think it's one hundred percent
Why we have mental issues
I feel mental health issues is that
I feel it's the stuff
That's going on inside
It's all happening
It's not getting spoken about
It's definitely the cause of it
Like, what else
It's experiences
It's trauma that's happened
It's the way they've processed
Some information
At some point in their life
There is something
That is the cause of that
Not having the chance to release
Not knowing how to release
People just end up breaking
And then that's when they say
Oh, that person's got
Mental health problems
Because they've done something
It has come out in some way

It's come out in some way where
People can then diagnose you
As being mentally ill
Otherwise they wouldn't even know
Something has happened
That has come out
Who says, that they've got
Mental health problems
Or they're mentally ill
Who decides and diagnoses
Just because
They're behaving in a certain way
If you just left everyone
To their own devices
And no one was policing everything
Maybe these people
Would do those things
And be okay
Maybe that was just a lash out
But in the way we have our structured
Constructed society
It's not the norm
It's not what you do
If someone starts running
Screaming in the street
Or smashing stuff up

Maybe that's what they needed
To be normal again
To be okay
But if they go and do that stuff
They're going to be locked up
They're going to be sectioned
Labelled, or whatever
That's the crazy lady.

LOVE & LUST AT FIRST SIGHT

It's more of
Liking the look of
It's more of an attraction
We can sugarcoat it
And call it all this stuff
But it's a physical attraction
It's like you look at someone
And you like the look of them
Either their face
They've got a nice face
It might just be someone's hands
That turns you onto them
Nice hands
Or the sound of their voice
It might be a telephone voice
You've never even met the person
There's always something
That attracts you
It may just be their body
It may just be a woman's booty
That turns on a guy
And then the rest follows
It may be just a woman
That likes a guy's face

Or his broad shoulders
Or something physical
Some attribute that is the attraction
And everything else
Follows from there
It can be lustful
A lot of the time it is
If we're talking about it seriously
It's a lust at first sight kind of thing
I don't know if I want to say
Lust at first sight
Is more accurate than
Love at first sight
More real
I don't know.

MENTAL STIMULATION

Good sex is important
And a stimulating mind
A level of intelligence
Someone I could talk to
Is important
How I feel right now
The latter
Would be more important to me
In getting myself
Involved with somebody
But there are other times
Where I felt like that didn't matter
I just want some good, good sex
And I've gone through phases like that
Throughout my life
Depending on where I'm at
And how I'm thinking
And what's around me
And how the stars are aligned
But right now
How I feel
At this very moment in time
And I've been feeling like this
A lot recently

It's mental stimulation
If someone can stimulate me
Mentally
That's my bigger turn on right now
Just because of where I'm at
I may be somewhere else next week
Or next month, or next year
But right now
At this moment in time
And recently
It's definitely been
Mental stimulation
That has been the thing for me
The thing that I'm focused on
I've been listening
To a little audio thing I have
It's like forty-five minutes long
It talks about sex transmutation
I've been heavily into that
At the moment
Because I find it an interesting topic
I've talked about it before
Just how you can transfer
That sexual energy
From having physical sex
Into something else

That may be considered more positive
Like some kind of endeavour
You may be trying to do
Whether it's creative
Or artistic
Or work related
Or starting a business, or whatever
How you can transfer
That sexual energy into that
And make that work
I have been
Very interested in that again lately
And the actual physical act of sex
Has not really
Played a role above that lately
It's been a kind of under thing
In fact, it's the complete opposite
It's taken that act of having sex
And transferring that energy
Somewhere else
So you're not actually
Going to have the act of sex
At this moment in time
Back to the question
It's definitely more the latter
Which is mental stimulation

That I'm more focused on
Rather than sexual stimulation
Although they can go hand in hand
But definitely more the latter right now.

ONE OF THE HIGHLIGHTS OF HACKNEY

She's this woman
I don't know how old she is
She frequents the Hackney area
That's where I live
So I see her quite often
Every time I see her
She's up to something
To be fair
And to her credit
I don't think she's mentally stable
Whatever that is
I think she has mental health issues
I always see her somewhere
It may be McDonald's
It may be on the road
She may pop into Gregg's bakery
I've seen her go into a vintage shop
And just walk out with what she wants
Basically, what she does
Is walk into these establishments
And basically helps herself
To what she wants
As if she's actually shopping
To pay for stuff

She'll see something on the shelf
But she'll take the third item in
Rather than
The first one at the front
Of that same item
She doesn't want that one
Or that one
She'll take this one
Like she's actually shopping
Purposefully picking out
The items she wants
But what she's going to do
Is walk straight out the door
And it seems there's nothing
That security or anyone can do
She'll be in McDonald's
And she'll be shouting
And cursing at people
She'll actually be screaming
At the top of her voice
For random people
To move out of their seat
From where they're sitting
I've seen random fights break out
And arguments
She just attacks anybody

Not physically attacking anybody
I haven't seen her
Physically attack anyone
But she definitely gets
Very verbally violent, let's call it
And just disturbs people
While they're eating their food
Picks fights with people
And arguments
I've seen things properly escalate
I haven't seen anyone draw blood yet
But I've definitely seen
Raised tensions
Where it could lead to that
The other day
I was in Greggs
And she walked in
She picked out a drink
She picked out this
She picked out that
And just walked out
Like it was nothing
Like it was on display for free
And the woman working there said
That they're not allowed
To approach her

Or try to stop her
Because she could have a needle
She could have anything
So they're not allowed to stop her
Another time I watched her
Walk into a vintage shop
Across from where I was
She went in there
And she walked out
With a bunch of clothing items
Still on their hangers
I saw this woman
Who worked there
Come out behind her
Talking to her
But not actually chasing her
Or trying to take the stuff from her
She just let her walk
And there's nothing she can do
She just goes around
And just helps herself to stuff
And abuses people
When she feels like it
I've just seen her today, actually
And she's got bags
She sitting by the wall

And stuff that she's taken
She has it on the wall
She got a pair of trousers
And I'm assuming
These pair of pink trousers
She's got spread out on the wall
Is something she has just
Acquired today, I'm guessing
That's what I'm assuming
She just does her thing, man
She's just like
A proper character around here
It's really bizarre
That's one way to put it, bizarre
She's always here
So obviously
She doesn't get in trouble for anything
It's just really interesting to watch
Even if she is apprehended, or whatever
Or caught, whatever
It appears that she
Won't get in any trouble
Wow, that's a bit of the life
Go into the shop
And help yourself
To anything you want

And walk out
And be good
And be cool
Like it's nothing
But it's the way does it
It's so calm
It's not like, Oh, I'm stealing
I've got to be kind of secretive
And duck down
And sneak out swiftly
She just strolls
Like it's acceptable to do that
It's funny to watch
Except that it's not funny
Because, obviously
She has mental health issues
But it's really bizarre, man
Yesterday, I saw her
She walked into McDonald's
I don't know if she knows the guy
I don't know, I'm not sure
But it didn't look like it
And she walked up to him
I don't know what she said to him
I was too far away to hear
But I noticed it

Because it was her
And she just took his burger
She took the whole burger
In the box
And was walking out
Passively and calm, he said
Can we at least share it
But she wasn't having it
She just walked out
With the whole box
And laughing
A few paces away from the door
And she was already eating it
She actually fascinates me
Her whole thing
Her whole way
It's amazing
It's amazing to watch
Obviously there's negatives to it
But man, it's something to see
She's always doing something
She's always upsetting someone
Telling them to move
If you're sitting in a certain place
That she doesn't want you to sit
She's going to tell you about it

And she's going to get very angry
She causes a lot of drama
She's a lot, man, she's a lot
Sometimes, I just like to watch her
She's interesting
She's very interesting
The things she does
And the way she does them
She's a character, man
She's an interesting character
So many interesting characters, man
If everyone was the same
It would be boring
She's definitely far from boring
She is not boring at all
She is one of the highlights of Hackney
She's a highlight of Hackney, man.

SEXUAL POLITICS

Once upon a time
I had five girlfriends
Like, you know, five decades ago
But not anymore
I'm pretty girlfriend-less
Like way girlfriend-less right now
I guess it's just how it is
I just like my own time
I'm quite an antisocial
Singleton, hermit
I'm a bit weird
A bit of a weirdo
It's just a lot of headache
Relationships
And girlfriends and boyfriends
And intimacy
And sex
And all that stuff
It's so much politics
So political these days
There's a reason
Why some people
Choose not to be
A part of that world

There's just too much
Politics involved
It's nice when it's nice
And you get along with someone
I like my own company a lot
And if I'm with someone
That's not complimenting that
My space
And what I like to do
And my time
And all that kind of stuff
It just doesn't work
Or I get too into them
And I get attached
And then it's like
My addictive personality takes over
And I want to be around them
All thc time
And then it just doesn't work out
And then
It affects me in a different way
It's just too much to take on
So I just don't take it on
I'm actually celibate right now
Sex is like
The last thing on my mind

And intimacy
And girlfriends
It's the last thing on my mind
It really is
I don't know if it's forever
But definitely for now
I'd like to think
That I'll experience sex one day
Down the line
But then, like I said
All the politics that comes with it
Makes it not worth it
It's nice, the idea of having sex
Getting down
Getting freaky
Enjoying yourself
Orgasm
All that stuff is great
Foreplay
All that is great
Getting naked
And rubbing skin to skin
And all the sexy, sexy stuff is great
But then
All the politics that comes with it
Makes you think

Oh, I don't want that part of it
I just can't be asked
So, it kind of puts you off
From a male perspective
Seeing what women get up to
And being on the outside
And all the stories
I see it all the time
I'm just not impressed
Not inspired, not impressed
There's no incentive
What other 'I' words
Can I think of
I just don't want to
Instigate anything
That will imprison me
I insist
Too much politics.

SHE LIKES IT ROUGH...ALL THE TIME

I had this one girlfriend once
That just liked it rough
That was her thing
She wanted it rough all the time
And I didn't
I didn't like that
That didn't do anything for me
That didn't make me look forward
To sex with her
So I learned that much about myself
I don't like it rough all the time
Or most of the time
And there's a limit to my roughness
If I'm going to go rough
She just wanted it rough
Hardcore
All the time
No sensual, slow
Slow down zone
She wasn't into that
So I learned
That I'm not cut out for that
I'm not into that
I like lovemaking

Slow down zone
Soft music
And you can ramp it up
You can take it up a bit
You can take it down a bit
You can play with it
But she just wanted it straight rough
Hardcore
Give it to me
Every time
Proper full on
I imagine there are reasons
Or a reason
To why she wanted it like that
All the time
But we never discussed it
We never had the discussion
But I know
That we would have had a lot more sex
If we matched more in that department
For sure
We just weren't compatible
In that department
I can go up to that, of course
But it's not where I rest
Her resting place

Is at hardcore rough
Give it to me hard
All the time
That's where she sits comfortably
I sit comfortably
More at some lovemaking
Sensual stuff
Stimulate you
That kind of stuff
Not like pow, pow, pow, pow, pow
So that's where I sit
And I could go up
If I'm in that mood
But she was up there all the time
All the time.

STRIP JOINT

It's not really my thing
I'll be honest with you
I'd probably go to a strip joint
And have a good old lap dance done for me
Just to say I've experienced that
I haven't before
But I would do it
Just to say I've had the experience
I'm all about experiences
And things that haven't tried
Haven't done it
But would do it
Just hasn't happened yet
A sexy woman in a thong
Whatever it is they wear
Bum bum in my face
Dancing on me
And trying to turn me on
With whatever she's doing
And dancing on my lap
With her nakedness
And all the stuff that goes on
In what I mainly see in movies
And on TV

Yeah, I'd be up for that
I'd try that
I'd say I've had the experience
But it's not really my thing
I'm not itching to do it
If it doesn't happen, it didn't happen
But if the opportunity came up
And it was aligned
With where I was at that time
And what I was doing
I'd say
Yeah, cool
Yeah, sounds good
Let's do that
If I've got some free time
Or whatever
Yeah, I would do that
Absolutely
I wouldn't say no.

THE BEST & WORST BOYFRIEND

I notice everything
I see everything there is to see
I'm one of those
Attention to detail people
I will see things that have changed
I'll see it when a woman
Changes her hair
Or changes
Something about herself
A little tint
Or she's done her roots
Or she's done her nails
Or something
A lot of guys
Would not notice at all
But I scc cvcrything
I think I see
Too much for some people
In the past
I've been very attention to detail
And it's made women self-conscious
Because they realise
That I see everything
They may think

It's the slightest change
That I'm not going to notice
But I do notice
And then they get self-conscious
About every little thing
What they're doing
And what they're saying
And how they're dressing
And then it can cause
A bit of conflict
They're putting themselves
Under a microscope
Everything they're doing
Scrutinising
And that can be a bit difficult
Because then
They're creating things
In their minds
That are not there
So that can be
A bit of a challenge
Sometimes
But on the other hand
They will come to me
And ask me stuff
Because they know

That I'm seeing
Beyond the normal
Or beyond
The usual surface level
I can see everything
And I can give them
A wide perspective
And detailed advice
Feedback, and so on
So it comes
With its good and bad
Positive and negative
It's yin and yang
All about balance.

THE FRIENDS YOU DON'T NEED

Sometimes
Friends just quit on you, man
Sometimes, friends just quit
People who you thought
Were your friends
You find out
They're not your friends
It's like they've just stopped
In the middle of the road
Like midway
Jumped out of the vehicle
And said whatever they said
And just went off
Or maybe you were the passenger
And they just stopped the car
Dead in the middle of the road
You thought you guys
Were going somewhere
And they just stopped the car
Dead in the middle of road
Opened the door
And kicked you out to the curb, man
Or like those eject seats they have
In those cars you see in the movies

Where they just press eject
And you shoot out
Or like in those jets
You eject out of the seat
They just said, you know what
I'm kicking this person to the curb
For whatever reason
For whatever's going on with them
Just know
That if you haven't done anything
That you're aware of
Or to your knowledge
Don't sweat it, man
Don't sweat it at all
It's just life
It's just the way things go
And a lot of the time
It's just to do with
Where people are
At that moment in time
Whatever's going on with them
Most of the time
Majority of the time
Has nothing to do with you at all
If you're shocked
If you don't understand

You're just taken aback
Like, how did this just happen
Like, you've just been disowned
You've just been cast aside
You've just been dismissed
No calls returned
If you know
You haven't done anything
To cause that
You've racked your brain
Looking at other angles
Of why this person
Who you thought was your friend
Is suddenly not your friend
And basically has you like a ghost
Like you don't exist
Like you're not there
Like you never were friends
In the first place
If you know
You haven't done anything
Don't sweat it, man
Don't sweat it
Sometimes
People are just in their own space
In their own head

114

With things they have going on
It's just the way it goes sometimes
Don't sweat it
Maybe someone
Said something to them
Maybe they overheard something
But if it's that
If someone said something to them
About you
And that's made them react
In a way
Which means putting you aside
Not talking to you anymore
Just totally cutting you off
If they're not adult enough
To come to you
And say something
Or tell you
That someone
Said something about you
Maybe it concerns them
And they feel hurt by it
And they just want to cut you off
If they're not adult enough
To come to you
And say something about it

Then they weren't a friend
In the first place
And they're not worth
Keeping as a friend
Or regarding as a friend
Or even if it's something
In their own mind
That they've decided
Some conclusion
That they've come to about you
And something
You may have done
Or said
Or maybe not something
You've yourself has done or said
Just something they've come to
In their own head about you
Or how they feel
About themselves
Either way
No matter what it is
Bottom line
No matter what it is
If they are not adult enough
To come and have a word with you
And say something

Even if they're going to say
I've decided
That based on this
I don't want to interact
With you anymore
So I'm not going
To talk to you anymore
To be adult enough
And confront a person and say
This is how I'm feeling
In regards to you
And this is where I'm at
And then you could understand
Why you've been cut off
Or disregarded
Or cast aside
At least
You could understand then
But for someone
To not be adult enough
To come and say something
About something someone said
About you
Or something they're feeling
About you themselves
Then that is not someone

You want to be having
As your friend anyway
That's not a loss
That is a blessing
You have gained something there
You've gained the loss
Of something you don't need
In your life anyway.

THE SHEDDING OF THE FORTRESS

Absolutely I have, Yeah
Because I allow myself to
The same way I am right now
How I talk
When I express myself
On paper
On video
Or audio recording
Or whatever
I'm the same
When I'm with someone
That I want to express myself with
I'm trying to do that all the time
I'm trying to always shed
All the time
I'll tell you what I liken it to
I think I mentioned it before
But it's like an air balloon
All those things
That we grow up with
That weigh us down
The sandbags
Eventually, as you're going up
In the air balloon

You cut off the sandbags
And you go higher
Or in a different direction
I look at it like that
It's a guard
We have this guard thing
Especially when we go
Into relationships
Especially if you've been hurt before
You come in with a guard
You're not going to share
All your deep secrets
And deep feelings
About whatever you've been through
In your life
So there's going to be that guard
I'm aware of that
Because I know
That when we're both able
To do that comfortably
Our relationship is going to be
So much better
So I'm always going in
With that in mind
I am absolutely guarded
I'm a one hundred percent

A guarded person
And I know I'm not alone
What it allows me to do is
It allows me to not be so guarded
It allows me to let go of that stuff
I don't need to be guarded about
Because we have these things
That we guard
We build up this massive wall
And shut ourselves inside
Some fortress
And no one can get to us
And we don't experience
The outside world
Or life
Or what's around us
As well as we could
If we didn't have that wall
So for me
It's about taking away
All those bricks
That I've constructed now
And locked myself inside
And let myself out
Take that wall away
And just be free

That's what I've been working on
Because I've learned
That it's all really complete bullshit
I get it
It's self preservation
It's a self defence mechanism
That we've devised
It's a safety thing we've created
And often we're creating against
An army that doesn't exist
We're building this massive wall
Against an army
That's out to get us
That's not there
That may be there
But it's not there
Like just in case
I'm not telling you
Anything about me
Just in case
I'm not sharing anything with you
Just in case
I'm going to keep my cards
Close to my chest
Just in case you use them against me
It's about that

It's not willing to be vulnerable
Not willing to put themselves
In that situation
Where they can be hurt
Mentally or physically
Matters of the heart
The video talks
Allow me
To share some of that stuff
Because all the things that I feel
That I'm going to be vulnerable with
I am able to put out there
I'm shedding, shedding, shedding
So much
To the point whereas
There's nothing left
For me to be scared about
Because it's all out there anyway
The stuff we hold close
And don't want
Anyone to know about
I'm slowly, slowly, slowly
Letting go of that shit
Letting it all go
So that I can be free
I can't be free

If I'm worrying about
What everyone thinks about me
And trying to hold on
To all these things
That don't even mean shit anyway
Because everyone's got
All their own problems
And no one's perfect anyway
Everyone's got their own shit
To deal with
We hold on to it
And it doesn't even fucking matter
So, I'm getting closer
I'm getting closer bit by bit
Lighter and lighter
Just release, release, release
Got to let it go
Because we carry so much
We carry so much
From childhood
We're carrying
We're carrying, we're carrying
We're carrying
And that stuff gets heavy, man
You're a child
You got that stuff

And then you become a teenager
You've got that stuff
And then you become an adult
And you've got that stuff
And you're just carrying
You're adding to your bags
All the time
And that shit is getting heavy
Dragging that along
So when you can start
Opening your bags
And taking a few bits out
And you pick up your bags again
To walk
It's a much lighter feeling
Until eventually
Your bags are empty
Or almost cmpty
And you're way lighter
You're flying by then
And you're living a better life
You're feeling good
You've shed all of that stuff
We just carry so much
And a lot of it is hard to let go
I'm finding a way

To shed that stuff
And a lot of the sharing
I've been doing
Is allowing me to shed
A lot of that stuff
Stuff I didn't even know
Was in my head
I just start talking
And stuff comes out
That I didn't even know was there
That's how deep it is
We may even think we're doing it
And we don't even know
That we're not doing it
We're still carrying it
We don't even know it's there
It's at the back of our mind
Subconscious shit
That we've been through
As a kid
Or teenager
Or even an adult
We're carrying it
And we don't even know it's there
That's crazy
Imagine you've got weight

You don't even know
That you're carrying
You look in the mirror
And you can't see it
But it's there
And you're heavy
But you don't know
That you're heavy
Because you can't see the weight
And there's no scale
To measure it
So you have no idea
That you're carrying
All this shit around
And it's fucking up your life
And you don't even know
You don't even know
That you could be walking
Much lighter
You don't even know
That you could be walking on water
If you weren't so fucking heavy
With all that bullshit
You could be walking on water.

THE TIME I MADE A SEX TAPE

We went and stayed in a hotel
We were doing our thing
We had all the special stuff
The little trimmings and all that
I can't even remember
What the occasion was
But we were in this hotel anyway
It was the Hilton
We stayed in a few
But I think it was the Hilton
It was all nice, it was good
It was a really nice time
All sexy and everything
I remember room service
Coming to the room
We had things delivered
It was really cool
I think it was champagne
Or some kind of bubbly
And strawberries
It was really nice
I had the camcorder
I remember setting it up
There was a cabinet

At the end of the bed
To the left
After I set up the camcorder
I pressed record
Let it run
And we did our thing
And had a good time, man
This is a long time ago
But it was good
That was like my first porno
That I made
My first homemade sex movie
I was the director, the producer
And I was the actor as well
With my actress
Making a porn
That's crazy when I think about that
Likc how long
I've been messing around
With cameras
And putting myself
In the role, so to speak
Although that's the only one
I've ever made
Let me say that
And we sat back

And watched it afterwards
And picked it apart
What we liked
And what we didn't like
And got turned on by it
And did it all over again
Just because of what we saw
It was good stuff, man
I totally forgot about that
You could call that my early days
Of dabbling in video and film
Wow, look at that
I forgot about that
It was good though
Watching that video back
A few years after down the line
Because I never erased it
I kept it
And I used to play it back
And enjoy myself
Because I set the camera up
How I wanted it
And captured
What I wanted to capture
Us enjoying ourselves
And that entertained me

For quite some time
I couldn't tell you where it is now
It'll probably turn up on the internet
In a few years
It's probably disintegrated
It was way back in the day
Camcorder and actual tape
It has probably degraded
Disintegrated into nothing now
You'd probably play it
And would just be all fuzz
White noise
But yeah
That's a good memory, man
That's a good memory.

TIME OUT

I'm in the middle of a courtyard
I'm on the green
Laying on this tree log
I'm using my bag for a pillow
The weather is quite warm
And still
I feel like I'm suspended
In the air
Off the ground
I feel like I'm closer to the sky
And closer to the trees
It feels kind of strange
But really relaxing at the same time
I'm watching the trees blowing
And it's just nice
Just the warm air
And the people strolling by
From work
Or wherever
They're heading to and from
It's a nice vibe
Sometimes
You've got to take time out.

VISUAL STIMULATION

I like to see
I like to see things
I love that
That turns me on
I like when a girl
Is looking into my eyes
And I like looking
Into her eyes as well
And I like to physically
See her body
You can do it in the dark
With music on
And it's great
That kind of thing
Or low lighting
And all of that is kind of cool
But I really don't mind
Having full lights on
Where I can see everything
And explore
And see what I'm touching
And in certain positions we're doing
I can see her body
In the way

It's connecting with mine
It just adds
That visual stimulation
It's an added stimulation
To the physical stimulation
Touch is one thing
But then when you add
The visual to that
What you can see
And feel
That's like a whole other level
It adds to it
It doubles it for me
If not triples it.

WHEN HER ASS IS TOO TOO BIG

I used to say
When I was younger
The bigger the bum, the better
But older now
I wouldn't say that so much
The reason being
When I was young
And experimenting
It didn't matter so much
That I could barely
Get myself inside her
Because her bum was so big
From behind, or whatever
Or in general
It didn't matter so much
I was just experimenting
And having fun
And trying to do stuff
But as I'm older
And there's more thoughtfulness
In what I'm doing
And how I'm doing it
And the amount of time I'm taking
And attention I'm taking

It does matter
How big her bum is
If it's way big
Like a mountain
I'm talking, literally Kilimanjaro
And I'm just me, as I am
It's not going to happen
If I have to climb that
To then get myself in there
It's not going to be that great
I'd be exhausted
Before I get up there
Before I even get to do anything
Kilimanjaro is said to be
The tallest mountain in Africa
So if I've got to climb that size ass
To get down, excuse the pun
It's not going to be that fun
Because if it's bigger than me
It's great to think about
It was great when I was younger
That she's got a massive ass
That's going to be just great
But it's not that great
If it's too big
Like too too big

And too big
Is a lot for me to say
Because there's still a part of me
That says nothing is too big
But in reality
There is too big
Because it can restrict movement
And therefore, restricted movement
Is restricting enjoyment
And it can affect the level
Or the intensity
With which you can penetrate
That will take away
Some of the enjoyment as well
So is there a too big
Yes, there is a too big
But in the case of myself
What can I say
Yeah, there's too big
But not that often.

WHEN WE'VE ARRANGED TO MEET

I haven't called my friend
To confirm
That we're meeting here
Meeting this time
What I did on the day
Was got us both to repeat it
And say the time
And write it down, whatever
Make a note
To say, we're meeting on Tuesday
Shoreditch station for 1:30pm
And I even made
A little voice note of it myself
For myself
To have it in my head as well
So, I didn't call since that day
To say, are you still meeting
Can you still make it
I didn't do any of that
I just said to myself
I'm going to get myself together
I know this is the day I'm meeting
I'm going to turn up
So I'm just kind of here

Hoping they turn up right now
And I think that's how it should be
You make an arrangement
And you stick to it
God forbid you can't make it
For whatever reason
Then you say, ahead of time
Sorry, something's come up
I can't make it
Can we reschedule, or whatever
But other than that
If that doesn't happen
You're expecting the person to turn up
And they should be expecting
You to turn up
There shouldn't be
Any other conversation
Regarding the fact
That you've made an arrangement
To meet on that day
That's as far as I see it
I know people
Who will send a text
Just to say
Are we still on for today
Just to make sure

That they don't go up there
Or arrive
And be waiting for the person
Who is not actually coming
But then, that would be saying
That the person
Is not going to tell them
If they're not coming
That's saying
That the person
Is not going to tell you that
That you'd have to actually text them
To find out
That can't be right
Because they should tell you
You shouldn't have to text them
On the day
Or the night before
To find out
That should be expected
That if they can't make it
They should tell you
You shouldn't have to be texting them
So in my mind
When you've made the arrangement
And it's firm

If you're people of your word
You should both be there
You should all be there
That's how it should be done
Why are you texting the person
To ask them
Are we still on
You shouldn't be asking them
We made an arrangement
So as far as I'm concerned
We're still on
You haven't told me otherwise
I don't need to text you
That's how I see it
So I haven't messaged, or anything
To say, are we still on for tomorrow
Or today, or whatever
I've just got myself together
And I've turned up
Half an hour early
And I'm just waiting
I'm just chilling
And that's what it should be
That's what I think it should be
I expect to see you
I expect to see you turn up

You're in hospital
You broke your leg, or whatever
I want to know about it
You can't make it, okay, things happen
Sorry, that's unfortunate
You died
You got buried the week before
I want to know about it
I want to hear
Send me a message from the grave
We were the only ones that knew
That we were both meeting
And you died
I fucking still want to know
That you're not going to turn up
For this arrangement
That I'm getting myself prepared for
I want some word from heaven
I don't care
I want some kind of note
Send somebody to tell me
Even though
We're the only ones that knew
Send somebody to tell me
I'm wasting my time
Because you're not going to be there

Or make other plans
Because I'm not going to be there
I died the week before
I want to fucking know
Don't make me waste my time
That is it, man
Let's be better with each other
Let's be better with ourselves
Like, fuck.

WHY MOST RELATIONSHIPS DON'T LAST

A lot of people
Are in relationships
Where they can't even talk
About their deepest feelings
That's crazy, right
A lot of people
We know this
The people they live with
They can't talk about how they feel
Partners can't express how they feel
About their parents
Because of how their relationship is
And they know
That they will be judged
Even though
They're in the relationship
With that person
It should be that person
That significant one
That one you hold close
Hold dear
Your lover
Your partner
Your everything

That should be the person
You should be able to go to
And talk to
About anything you're feeling
Any issues
Any problems
Whatever is going on
You had a bad day at work
Or whatever it might be
It should be that way
One hundred percent
But it's not always that way at all
It's absolutely no way that way
For everybody
There's people in relationships
Where it should be that way
And it's not
They're not getting that outlct
From their partner
They're not getting
That sounding board
They need to de-stress
And let it all out
And cry
Whatever it might be
Complain

That partner
Is not the person
They do that with
Because, for whatever reason
There's something there
That doesn't allow them
To freely do that
Whether it's the partner's fault
Or it's their own fault
There is definitely
Not that situation for everybody
There are people
Going through situations
But they have it all pent up inside
And the relationship breaks down
Because that's one of the factors
Where relationships break down
Because people
Can't express themselves
And be their whole self
And express how they really feel
Or they end up
Going with someone else
That they can
Share their deep feelings with
They have someone at that work

That does have an ear
And listens
It's just not that way
That is the ideal way
But it's just not
That way for everybody
Some people
Are in a relationship for years
And never really had
A proper conversation
About their childhood
Or growing up
Or why
They think the way they think
Or behave the way they behave
Because they just haven't had that
With that person
Unfortunately
Those things
We carry from childhood
That weigh us down
When you're with a partner
You're supposed to be able
To talk about those things
And let them out
Especially if you've never

Let them out to anyone before
That should be the person
That you let those things out to
Those things you need to release
That give you that light feeling of
I've shared this with somebody
I've got it off my chest
But it's not always the case
People are not always
In relationships
With people
Where they feel
Comfortable enough
To do that
They should do
But it's just not always the case
You hear people talk about it
A girlfriend
Will talk to her girlfriends
More than she talks to her partner
About personal things
That affect her life
And her mental state.

YOU CAN HAVE ANY GIRL YOU WANT

Me and this girl
I can't even remember
How old I was
I was young
And I think
Something wasn't working out
Or there was some break-up
Or some argument we had
And I must have been
Really into this girl
I must have been
Moping around
Or something
Because my gran
I don't know how old I was
I definitely wasn't sixteen yet
I'll never forget my gran
She's the greatest
She just said to me
Something to the effect of
I don't know
What's wrong with you
I don't know why
You're so worried

About this girl
You can have
Any girl in the world you want
Any girl in the world
That stuck in my head
To this day
It definitely helped
It definitely
Got me on my feet again
She actually instilled in me
The fact that
I can have any girl I want
Why am I worrying
About this one girl
Either that or she just thought
The girl was shit
And I could do so much better
Who knows
But she definitely instilled in me
That I could do better
And I'm worrying
About someone
That I don't need
To be worrying about
And stressing about
And crying about

And moaning about
And moping about
That's what she said to me
You can have any girl you want
And she just put that in my head
She gassed me up
As they say these days
You can have any girl you want
Forget her basically
I wonder if
She just didn't think much
Of the girl as well
Maybe that's what it was
She didn't think much of her
I genuinely feel though
That she just didn't like
Seeing me down
About what to her
Was something so insignificant
And I'm this kid
Who's got my whole life
Ahead of me
Good looking young guy
Gonna kill all the women anyway
Why are you worrying
About this one here

Who is not even that much
Of a stunner at all
I'm so glad
She did that for me though
Because that helped me
A lot in life
In life in general.

YOU HAVE THE POWER WITHIN

I think
You can do
Anything you put your mind to
I think you can change
Anything about your life
And your habits
And your practices
And your thoughts
That you want to
That you really want to
You have the power within.

ABOUT THE AUTHOR

Phoenix James is an award winning Writer, Poet, Author and Spoken Word Recording Artist. He began performing his poetic words live on stages across the UK in 1998. His debut spoken word poetry album, *The A.R.T.I.S.T,* was released in 2000. His first limited edition printed collection of poetry, *To Whom It May Concern,* was published in 2003. He has toured and performed his poetry internationally since 2004. He has appeared in films, on television and radio shows, and collaborated with other artists, singer-songwriters, actors, musicians, filmmakers and producers. In 2013, he wrote, directed and produced the feature length mock documentary film, *Love Freely but Pay for Sex.* Phoenix James is the author of several poetry collections and has recorded and released several spoken word poetry albums including *Phenzwaan Now & Forever, A Patchwork Remedy for A Broken Melody, FREE, Haven for the Tormented, With All That Said, Light Beams from the Void,* and over sixty spoken word poetry singles. All are available online now and streaming everywhere worldwide.

If you enjoyed reading this book, please leave a review or comment online. The author reads every review and they help new readers discover his work.

PHOENIX JAMES

Photo by Phoenix James

Phoenix James lives in London, England.

Connect with Phoenix James on his online social media platforms via www.linktr.ee/ Phoenix_James and say you've read this book. To contact or learn more about Phoenix James and his creative journey or to receive updates via his Newsletter Mailing List, visit his official website at www.PhoenixJamesOfficial.com

Phoenix James Official